Causes of Drug Use

DRUG ADDICTION AND RECOVERY

Causes of Drug Use

Michael Centore

SERIES CONSULTANT
SARA BECKER, Ph.D.
Brown University School of Public Health
Warren Alpert Medical School

MASON CREST

Mason Crest
450 Parkway Drive, Suite D
Broomall, PA 19008
www.masoncrest.com

MTM Publishing, Inc.
www.mtmpublishing.com

President: Valerie Tomaselli
Vice President, Book Development: Hilary Poole
Designer: Annemarie Redmond
Copyeditor: Peter Jaskowiak
Editorial Assistant: Andrea St. Aubin

Series ISBN: 978-1-4222-3598-0
Hardback ISBN: 978-1-4222-3600-0
E-Book ISBN: 978-1-4222-8244-1

Library of Congress Cataloging-in-Publication Data
Names: Centore, Michael, 1980- author.
Title: Causes of drug use / by Michael Centore.
Description: Broomall, PA : Mason Crest, [2017] | Series: Drug addiction and
    recovery | Includes index.
Identifiers: LCCN 2016003946| ISBN 9781422236000 (hardback) | ISBN
    9781422235980 (series) | ISBN 9781422282441 (ebook)
Subjects: LCSH: Drug addiction—Juvenile literature. | Drug abuse—Juvenile
    literature.
Classification: LCC RC564.3 .C458 2017 | DDC 362.29—dc23
LC record available at http://lccn.loc.gov/2016003946

Printed and bound in the United States of America.

First printing
9 8 7 6 5 4 3 2 1

TABLE OF CONTENTS

Key Icons to Look for:

Words to Understand: These words with their easy-to-understand definitions will increase the reader's understanding of the text, while building vocabulary skills.

Sidebars: This boxed material within the main text allows readers to build knowledge, gain insights, explore possibilities, and broaden their perspectives by weaving together additional information to provide realistic and holistic perspectives.

Research Projects: Readers are pointed toward areas of further inquiry connected to each chapter. Suggestions are provided for projects that encourage deeper research and analysis.

Text-Dependent Questions: These questions send the reader back to the text for more careful attention to the evidence presented there.

Educational Videos: Readers can view videos by scanning our QR codes, providing them with additional educational content to supplement the text. Examples include news coverage, moments in history, speeches, iconic sports moments and much more!

Series Glossary of Key Terms: This back-of-the-book glossary contains terminology used throughout the series. Words found here increase the reader's ability to read and comprehend higher-level books and articles in this field.

SERIES INTRODUCTION

Many adolescents in the United States will experiment with alcohol or other drugs by time they finish high school. According to a 2014 study funded by the National Institute on Drug Abuse, about 27 percent of 8th graders have tried alcohol, 20 percent have tried drugs, and 13 percent have tried cigarettes. By 12th grade, these rates more than double: 66 percent of 12th graders have tried alcohol, 50 percent have tried drugs, and 35 percent have tried cigarettes.

Adolescents who use substances experience an increased risk of a wide range of negative consequences, including physical injury, family conflict, school truancy, legal problems, and sexually transmitted diseases. Higher rates of substance use are also associated with the leading causes of death in this age group: accidents, suicide, and violent crime. Relative to adults, adolescents who experiment with alcohol or other drugs progress more quickly to a full-blown substance use disorder and have more co-occurring mental health problems.

The National Survey on Drug Use and Health (NSDUH) estimated that in 2015 about 1.3 million adolescents between the ages of 12 and 17 (5 percent of adolescents in the United States) met the medical criteria for a substance use disorder. Unfortunately, the vast majority of these

IF YOU NEED HELP NOW . . .

SAMHSA's National Helpline provides referrals for mental-health or substance-use counseling.
1-800-662-HELP (4357) or https://findtreatment.samhsa.gov

SAMHSA's National Suicide Prevention Lifeline provides crisis counseling by phone or online, 24-hours-a-day and 7 days a week.
1-800-273-TALK (8255) or http://www.suicidepreventionlifeline.org

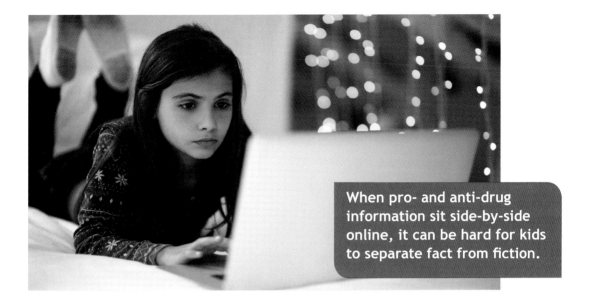

When pro- and anti-drug information sit side-by-side online, it can be hard for kids to separate fact from fiction.

adolescents did not receive treatment. Less than 10 percent of those with a diagnosis received specialty care, leaving 1.2 million adolescents with an unmet need for treatment.

The NSDUH asked the 1.2 million adolescents with untreated substance use disorders why they didn't receive specialty care. Over 95 percent said that they didn't think they needed it. The other 5 percent reported challenges finding quality treatment that was covered by their insurance. Very few treatment providers and agencies offer substance use treatment designed to meet the specific needs of adolescents. Meanwhile, numerous insurance plans have "opted out" of providing coverage for addiction treatment, while others have placed restrictions on what is covered.

Stigma about substance use is another serious problem. We don't call a person with an eating disorder a "food abuser," but we use terms like "drug abuser" to describe individuals with substance use disorders. Even treatment providers often unintentionally use judgmental words, such as describing urine screen results as either "clean" or "dirty." Underlying this language is the idea that a substance use disorder is some kind of moral failing or character flaw, and that people with these disorders deserve blame or punishment for their struggles.

And punish we do. A 2010 report by CASA Columbia found that in the United States, 65 percent of the 2.3 million people in prisons and jails met medical criteria for a substance use disorder, while another 20 percent had histories of substance use disorders, committed their crimes while under the influence of alcohol or drugs, or committed a substance-related crime. Many of these inmates spend decades in prison, but only 11 percent of them receive any treatment during their incarceration. Our society invests significantly more money in punishing individuals with substance use disorders than we do in treating them.

At a basic level, the ways our society approaches drugs and alcohol— declaring a "war on drugs," for example, or telling kids to "Just Say No!"— reflect a misunderstanding about the nature of addiction. The reality is that addiction is a disease that affects all types of people—parents and children, rich and poor, young and old. Substance use disorders stem from a complex interplay of genes, biology, and the environment, much like most physical and mental illnesses.

The way we talk about recovery, using phrases like "kick the habit" or "breaking free," also misses the mark. Substance use disorders are chronic, insidious, and debilitating illnesses. Fortunately, there are a number of effective treatments for substance use disorders. For many patients, however, the road is long and hard. Individuals recovering from substance use disorders can experience horrible withdrawal symptoms, and many will continue to struggle with cravings for alcohol or drugs. It can be a daily struggle to cope with these cravings and stay abstinent. A popular saying at Alcoholics Anonymous (AA) meetings is "one day at a time," because every day of recovery should be respected and celebrated.

There are a lot of incorrect stereotypes about individuals with substance use disorders, and there is a lot of false information about the substances, too. If you do an Internet search on the term "marijuana," for instance, two top hits are a web page by the National Institute on Drug Abuse and a page operated by Weedmaps, a medical and recreational marijuana dispensary. One of these pages publishes scientific information and one publishes pro-marijuana articles. Both pages have a high-quality, professional appearance. If you had never heard of either organization, it would be hard to know which to trust. It can be really difficult for the average person, much less the average teenager, to navigate these waters.

The topics covered in this series were specifically selected to be relevant to teenagers. About half of the volumes cover the types of drugs that they are most likely to hear about or to come in contact with. The other half cover important issues related to alcohol and other drug use (which we refer to as "drug use" in the titles for simplicity). These books cover topics such as the causes of drug use, the influence of drug use on the family, drug use and the legal system, drug use and mental health, and treatment options. Many teens will either have personal experience with these issues or will know someone who does.

This series was written to help young people get the facts about common drugs, substance use disorders, substance-related problems, and recovery. Accurate information can help adolescents to make better decisions. Students who are educated can help each other to better understand the risks and consequences of drug use. Facts also go a long way to reducing the stigma associated with substance use. We tend to fear or avoid things that we don't understand. Knowing the facts can make it easier to support each other. For students who know someone struggling with a substance use disorder, these books can also help them know what to expect. If they are worried about someone, or even about themselves, these books can help to provide some answers and a place to start.

—Sara J. Becker, Ph.D., Assistant Professor (Research), Center for Alcohol and Addictions Studies, Brown University School of Public Health, Assistant Professor (Research), Department of Psychiatry and Human Behavior, Brown University Medical School

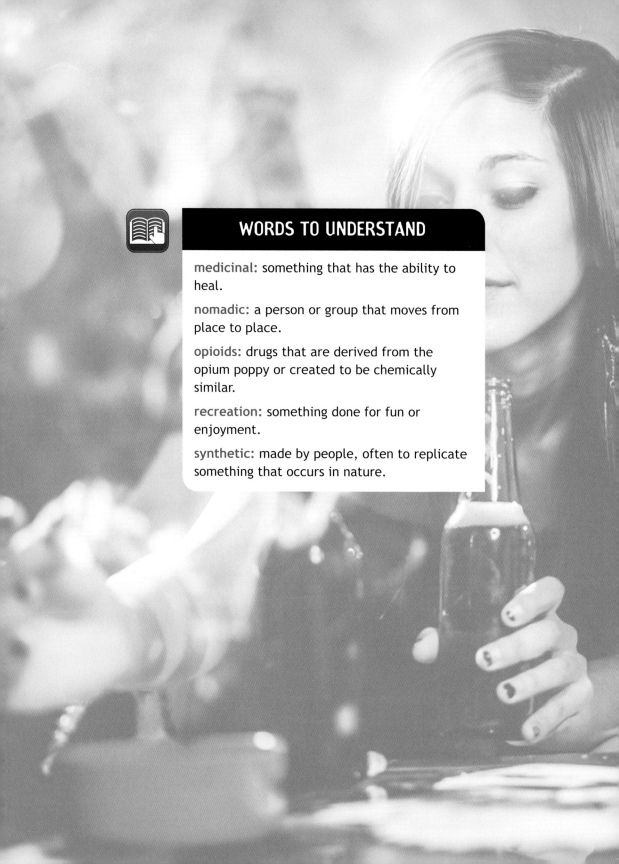

WORDS TO UNDERSTAND

medicinal: something that has the ability to heal.

nomadic: a person or group that moves from place to place.

opioids: drugs that are derived from the opium poppy or created to be chemically similar.

recreation: something done for fun or enjoyment.

synthetic: made by people, often to replicate something that occurs in nature.

CHAPTER ONE

DRUGS THROUGHOUT HISTORY

Whether they are prescribed for pain, carried illegally across international lines, or found in something as simple as a cup of coffee, drugs play a huge role in our culture. Debates rage about the function, legality, and potential dangers of drugs, and it can be difficult to separate myths from facts about specific drugs. It can also be hard to understand the difference between occasional drug use and a full-blown substance use disorder. In an attempt to keep kids from experimenting with dangerous substances, adults sometimes end up sounding like car alarms gone berserk—the louder they shout, the less any teenager wants to listen. Learning the facts about various types of drugs and the history of drug use is an important first step in making wise, safe choices.

In a 2014 national survey, 37.4 percent of 12th graders reported having used alcohol in the previous month. This was down from 43.5 percent in 2009.

DRUGS: AN OVERVIEW

A drug is a medicine or other substance that has a physical effect when introduced into the body. There are eight main types of drugs, some legal and others illegal: *stimulants*, which raise the activity of the nervous system; *depressants*, which suppress the activity of the nervous system; *hallucinogens*, which distort one's perceptions of reality; *cannabis* (or *marijuana*), a plant that has similarities to both stimulants and hallucinogens; *pain relievers*, sometimes called opioids, which are used to manage pain; *inhalants*, or toxic vapors from gases or liquids that cause disorientation; *performance-enhancing drugs*, taken to ramp up athletic performance and increase muscle mass; and *prescription drugs*, which are prescribed by a doctor or physician to help patients deal with medical conditions.

Drugs taken as medication are usually prescribed to relieve pain or treat infections or diseases. But some drugs are also taken for recreation, with no real medical purpose. Instead, they are taken purely for pleasure or to achieve a desired mood or state of mind. Both medicinal and recreational drugs can be misused, and both can lead to full-blown addiction. In fact, prescription painkillers such as Vicodin may be more addictive than many nonprescription drugs.

In addition to painkillers, other drugs commonly taken for recreation include cannabis, cocaine, alcohol, nicotine, caffeine, heroin, and hallucinogens such as LSD or mushrooms. Other drugs, including amphetamines or steroids, are sometimes used to enhance athletic performance. Some recreational drugs, such as alcohol and caffeine, which are extremely common in our culture, are often used in social settings. An important thing to understand is that just because these drugs are more socially acceptable than others doesn't mean they are less addictive or dangerous. For example, more than 8,000 people in the United States

INHALANTS

Inhalants are substances that, when inhaled, affect the chemistry of the brain. Common inhalants include glue, paint, shoe polish, gasoline, and nitrous oxide (otherwise known as laughing gas). Because they are cheap and easy to get ahold of, inhalants are a commonly used recreational drug among young people. They give users an intense but incredibly risky "high." Inhaling these chemicals reduces the flow of oxygen to the brain, which can cause serious brain damage or death after just one use.

died from heroin-related overdoses in 2013, but alcohol claims the lives of almost 11 times that amount, or 88,000 every year.

THE CULTURAL HISTORY OF DRUG USE

For as long as humans have been on the planet, they have been experimenting with mind-altering substances. Evidence suggests that Stone Age peoples of present-day Iraq used an evergreen plant called ephedra to ward off sickness as early as 58,000 BCE. As humans transitioned from a nomadic to a settled existence around 10,000 BCE, they began to grow cereals and other grains. They later found they could turn these crops into alcoholic beverages. Sumerians, members of the ancient civilization of Sumer in what is today Iraq, were brewing beer by 5,000 BCE. The production of wine, fermented from grapes, also increased throughout the Middle East around this time.

Cannabis—otherwise known as marijuana—was first grown in Central Asia, and production had spread to Europe by 2,000 BCE. It was consumed during religious rituals as a spiritual sacrament. Cannabis was also used in surgeries and other medical procedures to help control pain. When it wasn't being consumed, its tough fibers were strong enough to weave into rope, or hemp.

Across the Atlantic, Native American cultures were utilizing a different variety of crops. Plants such as coca (which is used to make cocaine) and tobacco grew in both North and South America, and people chewed them for their stimulating properties. When European explorers arrived in the 15th century, they discovered these products and brought them back to their native countries.

Tobacco became the most important cash crop of early colonial America. Around 1614, a settler at the Jamestown colony in Virginia named John Rolfe sent 4,000 pounds of it back to England. It became very popular there, and by 1630 over 1.5 million pounds were exported. The trade was so profitable some settlers didn't even want to grow food

This illustration shows different steps in the process of tobacco creation in the 1700s.

anymore! The colonial government responded with a law that made every farmer grow a certain amount of corn in addition to the moneymaking tobacco crop.

In the 17th and 18th centuries, trade expanded. Substances such as opium became more readily available. In addition, people began manufacturing stronger versions of particular drugs. What started out as natural, plant-based products used as "folk remedies" now acquired a new intensity. Distilled spirits such as gin provided a potent alternative to beer; cocaine synthesized from the coca plant provided a much stronger effect; and tobacco, previously chewed or snorted as snuff, was now rolled into cigarette form and taken directly into the lungs. These factors led to a rise in substance misuse throughout the world.

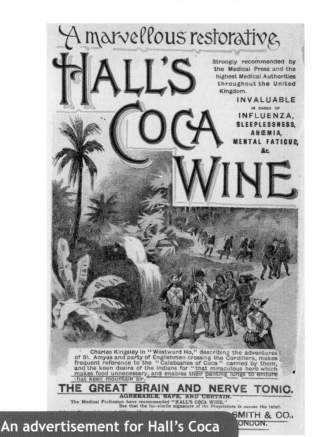

An advertisement for Hall's Coca Wine from the late 19th century. This "tonic" was made from the coca plant, just as cocaine is.

This trend continued over time. The more people discovered the properties of natural drugs, the more they were interested in manufacturing drugs with similar properties. These synthetic drugs are usually as addictive as naturally occurring substances, and sometimes more so. Their misuse presents a great threat to public health.

A modern-day example of this is the rise of "synthetic marijuana," or "spice," which

EPHEDRA TO EPHEDRINE

Drugs have a long history of being used in religious rituals. Priests or tribal leaders known as shamans, common in many different cultures, were known to use plant-based substances to communicate with spirits. In North America, the indigenous peoples of Mexico would ingest peyote—a cactus containing a hallucinogen called mescaline—to induce a meditative state. Soma, a drink that was probably made from a plant called ephedra, was a major part of the religious ceremonies of ancient India. It is still used in traditional Chinese medicine.

The active ingredient of the ephedra plant is called ephedrine. It's been used in modern times, too, since it's known to improve breathing,

stimulate the mind, and decrease appetite. Until 2004 it was marketed as a weight-loss supplement, but when users began to experience serious side effects, such as heart attacks and strokes, the U.S. Food and Drug Administration (FDA) banned it for this purpose. Ephedrine is also banned by many major sports organizations, including the National Collegiate Athletic Association (NCAA), Major League Baseball (MLB), and the Professional Golfers' Association (PGA).

The ephedra plant plays a role in traditional Chinese medicine, but it's banned from most professional sports.

Synthetic marijuana.

is often sold at gas stations or convenience stores. Producers are able to sidestep drug laws by changing the chemical formulas of the product and labeling it as "herbal incense" or "plant food." Unlike marijuana, which comes from a plant, synthetic marijuana is made from chemical compounds sprayed onto dried plant material. Because it is designed specifically for the human brain, its effects are stronger and the potential for addiction is much higher. (For more on this topic, see the volume *Marijuana and Synthetics* in this set.)

ADOLESCENCE: A KEY PERIOD OF RISK

Early adolescence is one of the highest risk periods for substance use. A 2011 report by the Center for Addiction and Substance Abuse at Columbia University showed that 90 percent of Americans with substance use disorders began smoking, drinking, or taking other drugs before age 18. The study also showed that 1 in 4 Americans who struggle with addiction began using substances before age 18. By contrast, only 1 in 25 Americans with an addiction began using after age 21. In the next chapter, we'll see why drugs have such strong effects on adolescent brains.

TEXT-DEPENDENT QUESTIONS

1. What are the major types of drugs, and what are their general effects?
2. What are some ways the production and consumption of drugs have changed over time, and how have these changes impacted public health?
3. How are synthetic drugs different from plant-based drugs? Include examples of each in your response.

RESEARCH PROJECT

Research drug use in various parts of the world. Write a brief report on your findings, including what factors (economic, geographic, cultural, etc.) contribute to drug use, the prevalence of certain drugs by region, and some of the ways different countries deal with drug use disorders.

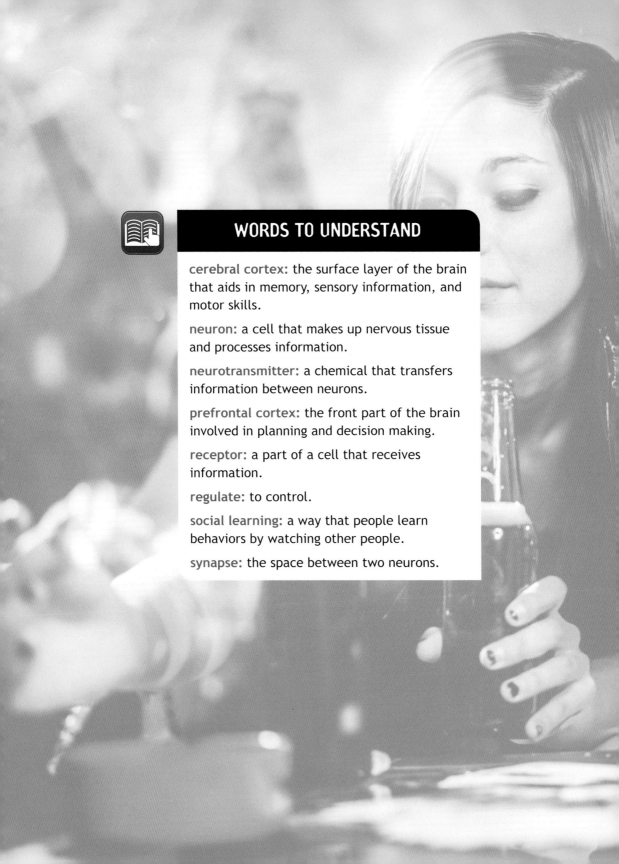

WORDS TO UNDERSTAND

cerebral cortex: the surface layer of the brain that aids in memory, sensory information, and motor skills.

neuron: a cell that makes up nervous tissue and processes information.

neurotransmitter: a chemical that transfers information between neurons.

prefrontal cortex: the front part of the brain involved in planning and decision making.

receptor: a part of a cell that receives information.

regulate: to control.

social learning: a way that people learn behaviors by watching other people.

synapse: the space between two neurons.

CHAPTER TWO

PSYCHOLOGICAL CAUSES

Psychology is the study of how the human mind influences behavior. It includes the study of how the brain works on a biological level, as well as how biology affects our experience. An incredibly complex system, the mind is where we store all our memories, thoughts, experiences, and beliefs. These all contribute to the way we act in the world. The relationship between psychology and drug use is complicated. There are many psychological reasons why people might choose to use drugs. In turn, drug use can affect the brain and affect how people feel. The next sections explore the ways drug use affects the brain, along with the psychological reasons why people might turn to drugs.

THE EFFECTS OF DRUGS ON THE BRAIN

The brain is divided into three main areas: the forebrain, the midbrain, and the hindbrain. The forebrain contains the cerebral cortex, which controls

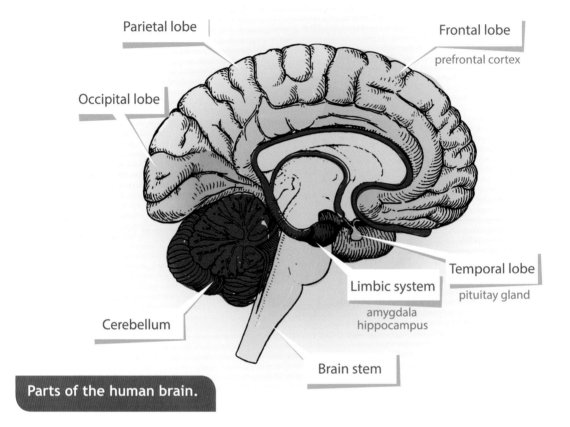

Parietal lobe

Frontal lobe

prefrontal cortex

Occipital lobe

Temporal lobe

pituitay gland

Limbic system

amygdala
hippocampus

Cerebellum

Brain stem

Parts of the human brain.

abstract thinking, problem solving, and decision making. It also organizes our thoughts and memories. The midbrain helps us build patterns of behavior that are necessary for survival, such as finding pleasure in eating food. The hindbrain is the "workhorse" of the nervous system and controls essential bodily functions such as heartbeat, breathing, and sleep cycles. The three parts of the brain stay in constant communication to manage bodily functions. This is done through billions of nerve cells called **neurons**. Neurons are the building blocks of the central nervous system of the brain and spinal cord.

Neurons send messages to each other through both electrical and chemical signals. When a neuron is stimulated, an electrical charge travels the length of its body. At the end of the body, the neuron releases a chemical called a neurotransmitter to communicate with the next neuron. The neurotransmitter moves across the space between the two neurons, known as a synapse, and attaches to a receptor in the receiving neuron.

There are many different types of neurotransmitters, and each type has a particular function. Specific neurotransmitters will only bind with specific receptors to ensure that the correct messages are communicated. Once the message has been sent successfully, transporters in the first neuron will "recycle" the neurotransmitter by bringing it back to the neuron. This stops the communication between the neurons.

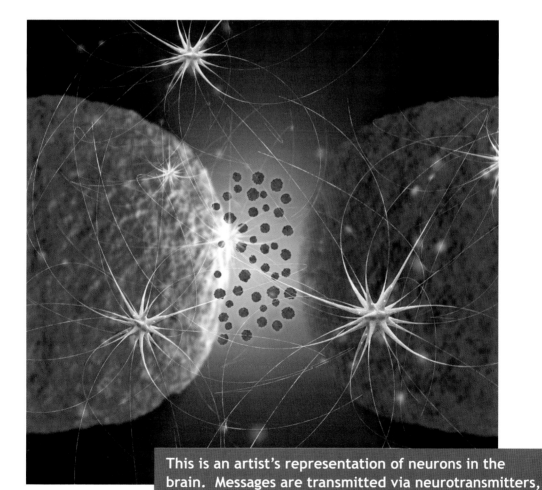

This is an artist's representation of neurons in the brain. Messages are transmitted via neurotransmitters, which are the red dots in this illustration.

Drugs act on the brain by disrupting these communication processes. There are a few different ways this can work. Drugs can mimic, activate, or block neurotransmitters, and they can bind to different receptors. For example, marijuana mimics a naturally occurring neurotransmitter and increases the activity of neurons in the brain.

Many drugs increase the amount of dopamine in the brain. Dopamine is the neurotransmitter that **regulates** pleasure and is responsible for feelings of happiness. The spike in dopamine levels that users get from drugs is what causes people to want to use again and again. Some drugs can release as much as 10 times the amount of dopamine into the nervous system compared with normal activities. This means that every time the drug is used, the association with pleasure is reinforced, and the need to use becomes stronger. Eventually, the craving can become so overpowering that it is beyond the user's control.

While drugs increase dopamine levels temporarily, they end up decreasing overall dopamine production and damaging brain circuits. That's because the brain becomes dependent on the drugs to provide surges of dopamine, and thus makes less on its own. The less dopamine produced, the harder it is to experience pleasure. This can create feelings similar to

THE LIMBIC SYSTEM

The limbic system is an important part of the brain to look at when talking about addiction. It's located in the center of the brain, above the brainstem and beneath the cortex. The system is a network of structures that process emotion, pleasure, and other primal feelings, such as fright or anger. Drugs can alter the processes of the limbic system. It begins to associate drug taking with the primary source of pleasure. This disrupts a person's emotional life, making it harder for the user to experience joy in other activities.

DRUG TOLERANCE

Tolerance is when the body becomes used to a substance, so that the user needs greater and greater amounts to achieve the desired euphoric effect. This can happen on a cellular level, when there is a decreased response to the substance after repeated use. It can also happen when enzymes (proteins that speed up chemical reactions and break down substances that enter the body) adapt to the drug. This wears down the drug's effects. Tolerance is not to be confused with addiction, even though people who develop tolerance to a substance can also have an addiction.

People sometimes brag about how much they can drink, but developing a tolerance to alcohol is actually an early sign of potential problems.

depression. Drugs can also impact brain circuits that control memory and learning. This can lead to reduced IQ and problems at work or school, as well as a loss of self-control.

All of these effects are particularly powerful for teenagers. Even though people are considered to be legal adults when they turn 18, the human brain is still developing until age 25. This has a few implications when it comes to drug use. First, any substance that affects the brain has the potential to cause long-term damage, and that risk is higher when growth is still happening. Second, the **prefrontal cortex**—which is the part of the brain handles planning, impulse control, and evaluating long-term benefits—is the last part of the brain to mature. That's why teens are more likely than adults to be attracted to high-risk activities that have short-term benefits such as drugs.

PSYCHOLOGICAL FACTORS

People use drugs for many reasons—to lower stress, manage pain, or forget a traumatic memory. Maybe they want to look cool or fit in with their friends. Sometimes they are just bored. Some people experience mental health problems such as depression (chronic feelings of sadness) or anxiety (chronic feelings of worry) and look to drugs as a way to feel normal. Others may see drugs as a quick way to change their mood or state of mind.

Drug use can also be what's called a "learned behavior." For instance, a person might start using drugs with specific friends or in specific situations and then learn to associate drugs with these experiences. If a teenager regularly drinks alcohol at parties with a group of friends, simply getting together with those friends could make that person want to drink. Even years later, a recovered user may still experience cravings when meeting up with those friends.

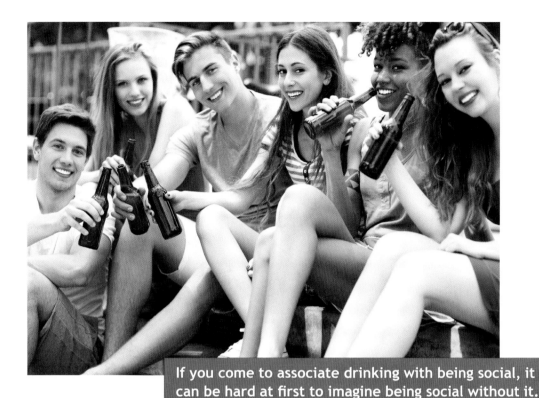

If you come to associate drinking with being social, it can be hard at first to imagine being social without it.

Young people imitate behaviors they observe in other people. This is a process called social learning. Watching family members, friends, or even actors and musicians use drugs can make people more likely to use, too. That's especially true if the people using the drugs seem happy and well adjusted, or if drugs are made to look glamorous. We often see images of people having fun drinking at parties, but rarely do we see their hangovers the next morning.

Drug use can move quickly from an experiment—trying things out once or twice to get the feel of the drug's effect—to a regular habit, problematic use, or full-blown addiction. A habit is a tendency or practice that is hard to give up, but that a person usually can control. Over time, habitual use can become problematic use if it starts creating issues with family, friends, school, or work. Problematic use can then become full-

WITHDRAWAL

Over time, drugs change a person's brain chemistry. When a person stops using drugs, it can lead to all sorts of emotional and physical complications. These are known as withdrawal symptoms. For some drugs, such as marijuana, withdrawal can be primarily emotional. This results in things like:

- anxiety
- insomnia
- depression
- nightmares
- anger or emotional instability

For alcohol or opiates, the effects can be more physical. These might include:

- difficulty breathing
- nausea and vomiting
- night sweats
- increased blood pressure
- rapid heartbeat
- shakiness or seizures

THC, the active chemical in marijuana, is stored in fat cells. Because of this, it takes much longer to exit the body than any other common drug, and withdrawal symptoms can last for months. Alcohol withdrawal symptoms can begin as quickly as two hours after the last drink and can last for several weeks.

blown addiction when it's very difficult to cut down or stop, even if the person wants to.

We don't know for sure why some people can stop at experimentation or at habitual use, while others end up progressing all the way at addiction.

The process of moving from experimentation to full-blown addiction is affected by both biology and psychology. As a result, it's still a difficult subject for scientists to understand. In general, addiction occurs when the brain begins to think it "needs" drugs, the same way it would need food or water. This is not only limited to drugs: people can become addicted to certain types of food, or even experiences such as gambling or exercise.

TEXT-DEPENDENT QUESTIONS

1. What are the three main parts of the brain, and what is each responsible for?
2. What are some reasons that people are driven to use substances?
3. How can substance use move from habit to addiction, and what role does the brain play in creating an addictive cycle?

RESEARCH PROJECT

Research a book, movie, or song that has substance use as one of its themes. Write a brief analysis of how this theme is portrayed. Is it a realistic account, looking at the physical and psychological costs of addiction, or does it make use seem desirable? Is its portrayal similar to or different from other works you have seen or heard?

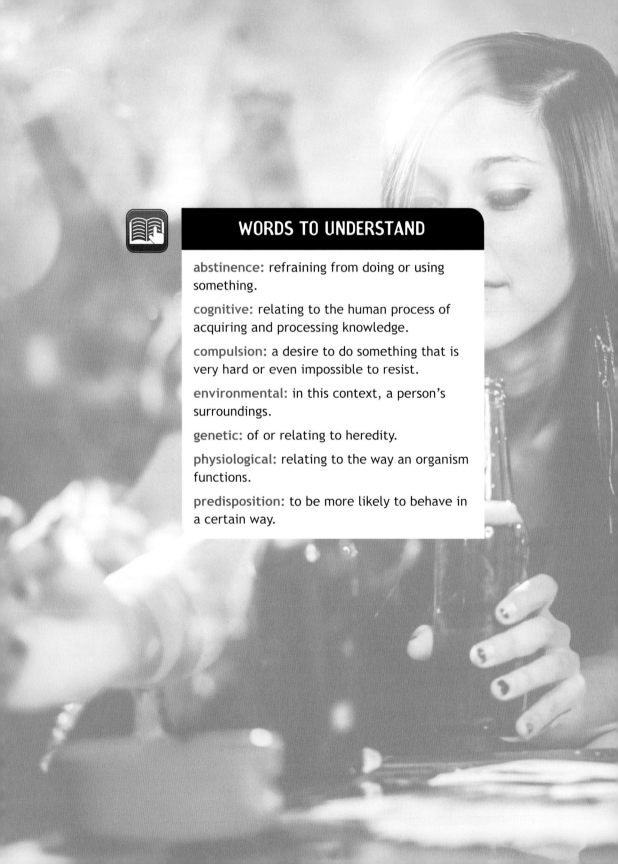

WORDS TO UNDERSTAND

abstinence: refraining from doing or using something.

cognitive: relating to the human process of acquiring and processing knowledge.

compulsion: a desire to do something that is very hard or even impossible to resist.

environmental: in this context, a person's surroundings.

genetic: of or relating to heredity.

physiological: relating to the way an organism functions.

predisposition: to be more likely to behave in a certain way.

CHAPTER THREE

GENETIC CAUSES

Genes are the basic units of hereditary information passed from one generation to the next. Whether you have blue or brown eyes, light or dark hair, or are taller or shorter than the average height of your friends are all determined by the genetic information you inherited from your parents. Genes are not only responsible for the way we look, but also the way we act and, to an extent, what we are good and bad at. In addition, genes play a role in our chances for developing substance addiction.

FAMILY HISTORY AND ADDICTION

The choice to use drugs is a personal one, but there are many factors that contribute. Environmental factors include how easily a person can access drugs, the attitudes his or her friends have about them, and what that person's home life is like. But it's not just about the person's environment. There are also factors specific to each individual, such as personality or a tendency to take risks.

31

Family history plays a big part in whether or not someone will experience substance use disorder. Children of parents with use disorders are up to eight times more likely to develop use disorders themselves. This is not due to a single gene, as it is with inherited illnesses like cystic fibrosis. Instead, addiction is the product of many different genes. For instance, genes that strengthen alcohol metabolism—the ability to process and eliminate alcohol from the body—may contribute to a person's tendency to drink.

The availability of drugs is one environmental factor that might make someone more likely to experiment with them.

STUDYING GENETIC CAUSES

To try and find which genes are responsible for addiction in humans, scientists experiment on mice, fruit flies, and other organisms. They then use this information to locate similar genetic traits in humans. Among their findings, scientists have shown that mice with limited serotonin (a neurotransmitter involved in regulating mood, appetite, and other brain functions) receptors are more drawn to cocaine and alcohol; that mice with a faulty gene called the PER2 gene drink greater amounts of alcohol; and that many nonsmokers have a gene that makes them feel dizzy and sick from smoking.

Another approach to the study of genetics and addiction is the study of twins. Identical twins share the same set of genes, while fraternal (or nonidentical) twins only share one half of their genetic material. Using this knowledge, scientists set up a "twin study" to find out how much of addiction is genetic. Looking at hundreds of pairs of identical and fraternal twins, they found that when one identical twin was addicted to alcohol, the other was likely to be addicted too. In fraternal twins, this similarity was not as common. This led scientists to conclude that genes are anywhere from 50 to 60 percent responsible for addiction.

Researchers sometimes study twins because they share the same genetic material.

Addiction specialists are doctors who have had special training in helping patients who are dependent on drugs or alcohol.

These genes are not always easy to identify, and because environmental influences are so complex, addiction can be tough to analyze. One thing is certain: healthy coping skills can overcome a genetic predisposition to addiction. Coping skills are learned behaviors such as relaxation techniques, the ability to recognize risky situations, and replacing cravings to use with healthier alternatives. Knowing this can give people hope that their fates are not determined by their genes alone.

IS ADDICTION A DISEASE?

A long-standing debate about addiction is whether or not it is a disease. Many doctors, counselors, and representatives from institutes such as the National Institute on Drug Abuse believe that it is. Like cancer or diabetes, addiction comes from a combination of genetic tendencies and lifestyle choices. In addition, as in the case of brain diseases, substances physically change a person's brain chemistry. They do this by mimicking neurotransmitters and distorting the brain's messaging ability, and by flooding the brain with dopamine. This disrupts cognitive abilities and can put the user's cravings beyond his or her control.

You might wonder why it matters whether we agree that addiction is a disease. A key reason is because, for a very long time, addiction was considered to be caused by a lack of willpower or a moral failure. If we understand addiction as a disease, it becomes easier to understand that people who suffer from it are not necessarily "bad" or "weak." Also, just like cancer or diabetes, addiction can strike people from all walks of life, occupations, and economic backgrounds. No one is beyond its reach. In fact, all humans are genetically programmed for addictive behavior— the repetition of pleasurable, life-preserving activities is how we've successfully evolved over time.

Environment, heredity, and coping skills all influence a person's chances of addiction. This complexity is what makes addiction so hard to predict. By understanding addiction as a disease and not a weakness, people with use disorders can begin to address the root causes of their problem.

ARGUMENTS AGAINST ADDICTION AS A DISEASE

While most scientific organizations are on the side of addiction as a disease, there are still contrary arguments. The most common is that the **physiological** changes brought about by drugs are not abnormal enough to be called a disease. Our brains are continually changing as they respond to new life experiences. Many activities other than drug use—such as conversing with a friend or practicing a new skill—can trigger a flow of dopamine and make us want to repeat the activity. Since we do not call any of these activities "diseases," critics say, we should not call substance use a disease, either.

Another argument against addiction as a disease is that diseases require medical intervention to be cured, but a substance user's brain can rebalance itself after a period of **abstinence**. In other words, you can't decide not to have cancer, but you can decide not to drink if you really want to. People may need counseling and other therapies, but they still have the choice to stop using. Those who say addiction is a disease argue that, no, some people actually *can't* decide not to drink—it's a **compulsion** rooted in genetics and brain chemistry.

CROSS ADDICTION

Because all addiction is rooted in the same part of the brain, people who are addicted to one substance can easily become addicted to others. This is known as *cross addiction*. It can lead to problems with relapsing, or

People in recovery need to be careful about substituting other drugs for the one they've quit.

returning to addictive behavior after a period of abstinence. For instance, if a person who has overcome a use disorder with cocaine turns to marijuana as a "substitute," it can trigger addictive tendencies that bring back cravings for cocaine.

Cross addiction doesn't just have to involve hard drugs. Addicts in recovery can abuse sleep aids or other drugs commonly available in pharmacies. It also doesn't just mean swapping one drug for another; cross addictions can develop around things like shopping or gambling, too. While cross addictions occur most often with people who are recently sober, and thus more vulnerable to the lure of substances, they can also develop even after years of recovery. Even if someone is no longer using hard drugs, cross addictions to other things can still have a negative impact on a person's life and family.

People in recovery have to take special precautions to avoid a possible cross addiction. For example, they might need to inform doctors that they are in recovery so they won't be prescribed any addictive drugs. Treatment for cross addiction can include behavioral therapy, in which a therapist helps someone recognize the thought patterns that are causing addictive tendencies, or stress-reduction techniques like meditation or exercise.

Dual diagnosis is a term that describes when a person has both a mental illness and an addiction. While cross addiction is not technically a form of dual diagnosis, the two concepts are similar in that the addict must be aware of how an addiction can influence other areas of his or her life. In dual diagnosis, this means that mental illnesses such as depression can trigger substance misuse, which can in turn reinforce a mental illness. It can become difficult to know which came first—the addiction or the illness—and so treatment is much more complicated. A person with cross addiction may not have a mental illness, but that person must deal with the threat of an addiction shifting to other substances. (For more information on dual diagnosis, see another volume in this series, *Drug Use and Mental Health*.)

Talking to others who are in a similar situation can be very helpful.

TREATMENT AND PREVENTION

Both sides of the addiction-as-disease debate recognize that substance use disorders will only stop when the user wants to change. The best remedy for use disorder is to understand the dangers of drugs and not experiment with them in the first place, but the causes behind addiction are not so simple. Preventative strategies such as school or community groups that inform people about the harmful effects of drugs are a good foundation for avoiding addiction. But when these do not work, a person who wants to overcome addiction must commit to replacing substances with new sources of happiness.

TEXT-DEPENDENT QUESTIONS

1. What is the difference between environmental and genetic factors when discussing the risk of addiction?
2. What are some key arguments for seeing addiction as a disease? What are some arguments against seeing it as a disease?
3. Do genetics entirely determine whether someone can overcome an addiction? Why or why not?

RESEARCH PROJECT

Research various treatment options for substance use disorders, including counseling sessions, 12-step programs, and long-term residential treatments. Write a brief summary discussing the methods each uses to help people overcome addiction, including whether they treat addiction as a disease.

WORDS TO UNDERSTAND

alleviate: to lessen or relieve.

hyperconscious: to be intensely aware of something.

interfamilial: between and among members of a family.

societal: of or relating to society, an organized social group.

temperance: avoiding alcohol.

CHAPTER FOUR

SOCIAL CAUSES

In addition to psychology and genetics, a person's family, friends, and cultural surroundings can all influence the possibility of addiction. These are known as *social causes*, because they relate to our interactions with other human beings. Observing a parent drink or use drugs, or seeing substance use portrayed as a harmless activity in movies or on television, can lead to experimentation and potential addiction. While the choice to use is a personal one, we don't often realize how much those around us shape our decision-making processes.

SOCIAL PRESSURES

We are all influenced by the behavior of our friends in one way or another. It's easier to justify trying something new or risky if you see someone else doing it. That's probably why peer pressure is one of the main reasons why teenagers and adults alike elect to use substances.

Right or wrong, teenage users are seen as more mature than nonusers by their peers—even if they're really immature in other respects. They have

41

the ability to get a hold of something dangerous and illegal, which gives them a sense of social status. Other teens who want to be seen as popular will experiment just to be associated with them.

There's a natural urge to want to declare your independence and break free of your parents' influence during high school. After years of having to wait on adults for rides, new freedoms like a driver's license can open up all kinds of social options. You're growing as a person, starting to find out what really interests you, and deciding who you want to hang out with and how you want to spend your time. Since access to and use of drugs and alcohol are signs of maturity, they provide a quick—if potentially dangerous—way of feeling more "adult." Instead of trying to dialogue with your parents about your need for greater freedom, it might seem easier to turn to drugs or alcohol as a way to assert yourself.

Lack of confidence is another reason some teens use substances. Because alcohol and drugs can free people of their inhibitions, they allow them to act in ways they otherwise wouldn't. Socializing becomes

Sometimes teens worry they'll be left out of their group if they don't go along with what everyone else is doing.

COMMUNITY SCHOOLS

Students who feel left out of their school environments are more likely to turn to substances. A new movement in education is looking to make schools feel more inclusive by thinking of them as communities

Do "community schools" foster improved relationships or just lead to more segregation?

instead of institutions. This means more student-teacher interaction, programs to encourage friendships between different students, and the creation an environment based on cooperation rather than competition. These "full-service" schools also seek to partner with local businesses, youth organizations, and health agencies from the local community. This helps connect the students to a wider network of people and opportunities for growth.

Although the community-school movement has the potential to do a lot of good, some educational professionals have criticisms. They say that community schools end up segregating students. This is especially true in larger urban areas, where for many years there have been efforts to integrate students of different backgrounds and communities. Those policies are reversed in community schools, because the schools seek to cluster students around their own neighborhoods. Since schools in wealthier neighborhoods often end up outperforming those in poorer (usually black and Latino) ones, the schools may reinforce old patterns of inequality.

LEADERS AND BONDERS

A 2011 study published in the *Journal of Early Adolescence* looked at how teens' social goals (like making or influencing friends) related to substance use. Within teen peer groups, leaders tend to be those who are perceived as the most adult-like. The study showed that teens who wished to be the leaders of their peer groups had higher rates of nicotine use, since smoking is seen as a "grown-up" activity. Teens who wished to fit into their peer groups preferred to experiment with alcohol, since drinking is seen as more of a "bonding" activity.

Alcohol is sometimes considered a "bonding" activity.

easier. Any misstep or embarrassing situation can be explained away with "I was so wasted." It's easy to be hyperconscious of how you appear to others, so the effects of alcohol and drugs can seem incredibly liberating at first. Different substances give different feelings of empowerment. For instance, alcohol and amphetamines allow someone to act on their frustrations aggressively, while marijuana allows them to withdraw into a conflict-free space.

THE INFLUENCE OF FAMILY

Beyond genetics, the influence of a person's family environment plays a huge role in determining patterns of addiction. Teens who witness a parent, relative, or elder sibling engage in substance use are much more likely to imitate that behavior. In homes where use occurs, substances are also more likely to be accessible, making it easier for teens to experiment.

When **interfamilial** communication is strong, there is less chance of teens developing use disorders. If teens are willing to ask their parents for information—and parents are willing to provide clear and direct answers—

Strong family relationships can help kids resist the temptation of drugs and alcohol.

THE TEMPERANCE MODEL

One way governments protect societies from the harmful effects of drugs and alcohol is by limiting access. Keeping the legal age to purchase alcohol at 21 and taxing cigarettes are two examples. Some substances, such as heroin, are banned outright for the public good. This is known as the temperance model of prevention. Between 1919 and 1933, the United States outlawed the production and sale of all alcoholic beverages, a period known as Prohibition. The law led to widespread bootlegging (when people made liquor, often of low quality, themselves), loss of tax revenue, and the growth of criminal organizations that supplied liquor illegally. People who argue for the legalization of drugs frequently use Prohibition as evidence that the temperance model doesn't work.

A poster from 1951 advertising "World Temperance Sunday" by the Kansas United Dry Forces.

kids often have less curiosity about substances and less of an urge to rebel. This doesn't mean that teens from homes with strong communication do not face temptation. But they are often better prepared to make informed decisions about drugs and alcohol when the time comes.

A more extreme case of familial influence on addiction is that of emotional, physical, or sexual abuse. Young people who experience abuse are more likely to turn to drugs or alcohol as a way to cope with their inner pain. This can turn into a habitual form of self-medication, in which drugs or alcohol are used to alleviate the stress of the outside world. Because stress causes the brain to produce more dopamine, even the memory of abuse can create long-term changes in brain chemistry and function, leading to possible substance use disorder.

If you or someone you know is a victim of any type of abuse, talk to someone—a teacher, family friend, religious leader, or any trusted adult—to get the necessary help. No matter what anybody says, you are not powerless to address the problem. Seeking refuge in substances will only add another level of suffering to an already traumatic experience.

COMMUNITY RISK FACTORS

After the peer group and the family, wider societal trends can influence drug use in teens. Among these are the way drugs and alcohol are portrayed in popular culture. If substance use is shown without showing the consequences, it can lead young, impressionable viewers to think they can experiment safely. Advertisers' marketing strategies to make alcohol and nicotine look attractive usually hide their many health risks.

Laws, public policies, and surrounding cultural attitudes are also important. For instance, in countries like Canada, where the drinking age is 18 (or 19 in some provinces), young people have easier access to alcohol. It is thought that over 80 percent of teenagers in Canada drink, which

BULLYING AND ADDICTION

Both bullying and gang activity are social risk factors for addiction among teens. Research shows that those who bully have a higher rate of alcohol use. To cope with the stress and fear of being bullied, victims have higher rates of substance use than nonvictims. Even more so than in peer groups, substance use is a part of the culture of gangs. Teens who lack role models or family structure may seek out gangs for a feeling of community, and thus open themselves up to the possibility of misuse and addiction.

increases the risk for alcoholism in adulthood. One recent study examined the causes of death of Canadians between 16 and 22 years of age. It found that immediately after the legal drinking age, male deaths due to motor vehicles spiked by 15 percent, while deaths due to injuries increased by 16

At the Montreal Grand Prix in 2012, a simulator showed people the negative effects of alcohol on their driving abilities.

percent. The study concluded that raising the drinking age to 21 would save the lives of about 32 young men (between 18 and 20 years of age) annually.

TEXT-DEPENDENT QUESTIONS

1. What are some reasons that teens are susceptible to peer pressure, and how does this affect their decisions about substance use?
2. What are some ways that family life might influence the possibility of addiction?
3. Does society play a role in an individual's ideas about substance use? Why or why not?

RESEARCH PROJECT

Research key aspects of the temperance movement and how it helped bring about Prohibition, then read a selection of contemporary articles about the movement to legalize marijuana. What are the similarities and differences between the two time periods and historical situations? Write a brief report summarizing your findings, being sure to explain why Prohibition is so often mentioned in the current debate on legalization.

WORDS TO UNDERSTAND

alienation: a sense of isolation or detachment from a larger group.

implement: to put a plan or decision into practice.

mitigate: to make something less painful or severe.

protective factor: behaviors, traits, or influences, that work against risk factors to guard against addiction.

risk factors: behaviors, traits, or influences that make a person vulnerable to something.

CHAPTER FIVE

PREVENTION

Substance use disorders do a lot of damage to societies. Use disorders can lead to heart disease, diabetes, and other ailments, not to mention the strain they place on families, communities, and workplace environments. Prevention strategies are the methods used to limit use disorders before they start, or to help people suffering from use disorders to change their behavior. By using prevention strategies, a community's long-term health can be improved.

BASIC PREVENTION TERMINOLOGY

Health professionals see prevention as part of a larger system of care. This incorporates promotion, prevention, treatment, and recovery. *Promotion* is making people comfortable enough to receive and act on counseling; *prevention* is the action taken to reduce risk before a use disorder begins; *treatment* is the series of steps prescribed for people who have use disorders; and *recovery*, or *maintenance*, is the process of helping people stay away from substances after treatment.

You don't have to "hit bottom" in order to ask for help with substance misuse.

Prevention itself is broken down into three levels, each for a different set of people. *Universal efforts* target all sorts of people, even those with low risk of addiction; *selective efforts* target those most at risk of substance use; and *indicated efforts* target those who already show signs of use disorder. Indicated efforts may overlap with an intervention, which is when a group of family members, friends, and health-care professionals confront a person directly about his or her substance use.

A person doesn't have to "hit bottom" in order to begin recovery. Among adolescents who are experimenting with drugs for the first time, an intervention is itself an addiction prevention strategy. This is because adolescents will most likely have only just begun using and are not yet in the full grasp of addiction. An early intervention can therefore help prevent addiction before it starts.

PREVENTION STRATEGIES: TARGETING RISK FACTORS

To determine a person's level of risk, both **risk factors** and **protective factors** are important. Risk factors are those behaviors, traits, or family or social characteristics that leave someone vulnerable to substance use disorder. Protective factors are those qualities which mitigate risk factors. For example, the protective factor of self-control guards against the risk factor of early childhood aggression.

The chance of a person having a use disorder is a blend of risk factors and protective factors. Prevention strategies aim to increase protective factors and decrease risk factors. Risk factors can be rooted in individual, family, or school and community backgrounds. Individual risk factors include low self-esteem, aggression, and lack of self-control. Family risk factors include parents who don't communicate with their kids or who discipline them too harshly. This can inspire kids to rebel, or it can damage their confidence, making them more withdrawn and more likely to want to escape through substances. Peer substance use, poverty, poor academic performance, and feelings of alienation from one's surroundings are all school and community risk factors.

Each of these different arenas—community, school, and family—provides different opportunities to address these factors. For example, universal prevention efforts aimed at an entire community may involve constructing billboards that point out the dangers of drugs, or implementing drug-

GROUNDED IN EVIDENCE

One trend in substance use prevention is the use of what's called evidence-based practices. These are prevention actions that have been tested with research and proven to work. Treatment centers want to be sure the practice has been published and reviewed in a scholarly journal, that it has a history of success, and that it can be easily repeated. Critics of evidence-based practices question whether they can be effective in the "real world" outside of research institutions, where people may need more personalized attention.

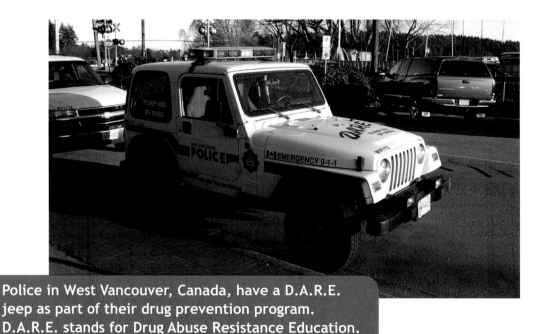

Police in West Vancouver, Canada, have a D.A.R.E. jeep as part of their drug prevention program. D.A.R.E. stands for Drug Abuse Resistance Education.

free zones around schools. Selective efforts based in schools might target populations that are most at risk with drug-awareness workshops, counseling sessions, or after school programs that help kids make new friends. Finally, indicated efforts at the family level may use therapy to strengthen family bonds and help teach parents the best ways to discipline their children.

OTHER PREVENTATIVE STRATEGIES: TAKING CHARGE

Of course, no matter how well thought out these preventative strategies are, they depend on people's willingness to listen and learn in order to succeed. One of the best methods of prevention is for young people to get informed about substance use disorders, then take steps to reduce risk factors within their control. Websites such as the NIDA for Teens "Drug Facts" section (http://teens.drugabuse.gov/drug-facts) are excellent places to start getting educated about the effects of drugs.

Going a step further, teens can challenge themselves to find productive activities that replace the easy escape of substances. Even something as simple as spending time with friends or neighbors, focusing on becoming a better athlete, or picking up a new hobby like music or dancing can go a long way in curbing the boredom and isolation that can inspire drug use. The rewards also last a lot longer than the temporary fix of drugs.

Peer-to-peer (P2P) prevention is when students, rather than parents, teachers, or other authority figures, educate each other about drug and alcohol use disorders. The thinking behind this method is that young people are more likely to listen to each other than they are to listen to adults. After initial training, "peer educators" help their classmates with mentoring, counseling, and providing information about substances.

There may come a time where you are called to help a friend who is struggling with addiction, much like an indicated prevention effort. Be prepared to listen and provide support. Utilize the NIDA resources mentioned above to school yourself in use disorders, and pass the information along. It may be overwhelming for both you and your friend, so

Sometimes peer-to-peer conversations are more effective than authority figures giving lectures.

LOOKING INWARD

One way to educate yourself on the ins and outs of substance use disorder is to study someone else's experience with addiction. "Addiction memoirs" are first-person accounts of the trials and tribulations of drug and alcohol use. The earliest example of the genre was probably Thomas De Quincey's *Confessions of an English Opium-Eater* (1821). The book details his experiences with laudanum, a combination of alcohol and opium. More recent memoirs include Jim Carroll's *The Basketball Diaries* (1978), which was later made into a movie, and Mary Karr's *Lit* (2009). Memoirs aimed at teens include two books by Nic Sheff, *Tweak: Growing Up on Methamphetamines* (2009) and *We All Fall Down* (2012), and Mary Rose's *Dear Nobody* (2014).

Books can help you gain insight into lives that are different from your own.

don't be afraid to reach out to an adult you can trust and ask for help. The website of the Substance Abuse and Mental Health Services Administration (SAMHSA) has an online database of treatment facilities searchable by zip code, available at https://findtreatment.samhsa.gov/.

MECHANICS OF A PREVENTION PROGRAM

The three basic elements of prevention programs are structure, content, and delivery. *Structure* addresses how the program is developed, thinking about the intended audience and environment. *Content* is the way that information, ideas, and new skills are presented to the audience. *Delivery* "tweaks" the program to best fit within different communities, seeking to provide the most necessary pieces of information.

The drug-prevention group Narcotics Overdose Prevention & Education (NOPE) makes for a good example of how these elements take form. NOPE is structured to target young people and their families in communities at risk for overdose deaths. It provides educational content about drugs, addiction, and treatment options through in-school presentations and online resources. It also brings communities together with events like candlelight vigils to remember those lost to substance misuse. Local chapters of NOPE tailor delivery of programs and content to best address the needs of their communities. While the chapters use many of NOPE's authorized materials, they incorporate local media, news articles, and treatment centers into their programs. They also advocate for drug education and reform by developing relationships with legislators.

TEXT-DEPENDENT QUESTIONS

1. What are the three levels of prevention and how are they defined?
2. What is the difference between risk factors and protective factors, and what are some examples of each?
3. In what ways can teens educate themselves about substance use disorders?

RESEARCH PROJECT

Research a substance use treatment facility or recovery center in your area. If possible, arrange a visit and a brief interview with a counselor to discuss how the facility works and what types of prevention strategies they employ. Write a report summarizing your findings.

FURTHER READING

BOOKS

Dolin, Eric Jay. *When America First Met China: An Exotic History of Tea, Drugs, and Money in the Age of Sail*. New York: Liveright, 2012.

Hornik-Beer, Edith Lynn. *For Teenagers Living with a Parent Who Abuses Alcohol/Drugs*. Lincoln, NE: iUniverse, 2001.

Lopez, German. "The Risks of Alcohol, Marijuana, and Other Drugs, Explained." *Vox Science and Health*, February 25, 2015. http://www.vox.com/2015/2/25/8104917/drug-dangers-marijuana-alcohol.

Rodriguez, Tori. "ADHD and Addiction May Share Genetic Basis." *Psychiatry Advisor*, November 12, 2015. http://www.psychiatryadvisor.com/adhd/attention-deficit-hyperactivity-disorder-substance-abuse-genes/article/453601/.

Sheff, David. *Beautiful Boy: A Father's Journey through His Son's Addiction*. Boston: Mariner Books, 2009.

Steiker, Lori Holleran. *Youth and Substance Abuse: Prevention, Intervention, and Recovery*. Chicago: Lyceum Books, 2016.

ONLINE

Addictions and Recovery. http://www.addictionsandrecovery.org.

Mayo Clinic. Drug Addiction. http://www.mayoclinic.org/diseases-conditions/drug-addiction/basics/definition/con-20020970.

Partnership for Drug-Free Kids. http://www.drugfree.org.

Substance Abuse and Mental Health Services Administration (SAMHSA). http://www.samhsa.gov/.

EDUCATIONAL VIDEOS

Access these videos with your smartphone or use the URLs below to find them online.

 "Why Are Drugs So Hard to Quit?" National Institute on Drug Abuse. "This video from NIDA explains addiction in simple terms and offers a hotline to help you or a loved one find treatment." https://youtu.be/zV6zKmt7S5E

 "The Reward Circuit: How the Brain Responds to Natural Rewards and Drugs," National Institute on Drug Abuse. "Learn about the limbic system and the biochemical processes that allow this key brain region to process rewards." https://youtu.be/DMcmrP-BWGk

 "Dr. Nora Volkow Explains the Science of Addiction," Office of National Drug Control Policy. "The Director of the National Institute on Drug Abuse at the National Institutes of Health describes the scientific foundation for the President's National Drug Control Strategy." https://youtu.be/JH7zq0_VA9U

 "Anyone Can Become Addicted to Drugs," National Institute on Drug Abuse. "This video from NIDA explains addiction in simple terms and offers a hotline to help you or a loved one find treatment." https://youtu.be/SY2luGTX7Dk

 "The Unyielding Power of Dopamine," Big Think. "Drug addiction researcher Nora Volkow walks us through the singular chemical that drives substance abuse." https://youtu.be/pUkrPNxLau0

SERIES GLOSSARY

abstention: actively choosing to not do something.

acute: something that is intense but lasts a short time.

alienation: a sense of isolation or detachment from a larger group.

alleviate: to lessen or relieve.

binge: doing something to excess.

carcinogenic: something that causes cancer.

chronic: ongoing or recurring.

cognitive: having to do with thought.

compulsion: a desire that is very hard or even impossible to resist.

controlled substance: a drug that is regulated by the government.

coping mechanism: a behavior a person learns or develops in order to manage stress.

craving: a very strong desire for something.

decriminalized: something that is not technically legal but is no longer subject to prosecution.

depressant: a substance that slows particular bodily functions.

detoxify: to remove toxic substances (such as drugs or alcohol) from the body.

ecosystem: a community of living things interacting with their environment.

environment: one's physical, cultural, and social surroundings.

genes: units of inheritance that are passed from parent to child and contain information about specific traits and characteristics.

hallucinate: seeing things that aren't there.

hyperconscious: to be intensely aware of something.

illicit: illegal; forbidden by law or cultural custom.

inhibit: to limit or hold back.

interfamilial: between and among members of a family.

metabolize: the ability of a living organism to chemically change compounds.

neurotransmitter: a chemical substance in the brain.

paraphernalia: the equipment used for producing or ingesting drugs, such as pipes or syringes.

physiological: relating to the way an organism functions.

placebo: a medication that has no physical effect and is used to test whether new drugs actually work.

predisposition: to be more inclined or likely to do something.

prohibition: when something is forbidden by law.

recidivism: a falling back into past behaviors, especially criminal ones.

recreation: something done for fun or enjoyment.

risk factors: behaviors, traits, or influences that make a person vulnerable to something.

sobriety: the state of refraining from alcohol or drugs.

social learning: a way that people learn behaviors by watching other people.

stimulant: a class of drug that speeds up bodily functions.

stressor: any event, thought, experience, or biological or chemical function that causes a person to feel stress.

synthetic: made by people, often to replicate something that occurs in nature.

tolerance: the state of needing more of a particular substance to achieve the same effect.

traffic: to illegally transport people, drugs, or weapons to sell throughout the world.

withdrawal: the physical and psychological effects that occur when a person with a use disorder suddenly stops using substances.

INDEX

ABOUT THE AUTHOR

Michael Centore is a writer and editor. He has helped produce many titles for a variety of publishers, including memoirs, cookbooks, and educational materials, among others. He has authored several previous volumes for Mason Crest, including titles in the Major Nations in a Global World and North American Natural Resources series. His essays have appeared in the *Los Angeles Review of Books, Killing the Buddha, Mockingbird,* and other print- and web-based publications. He lives in Connecticut.

ABOUT THE ADVISOR

Sara Becker, Ph.D. is a clinical researcher and licensed clinical psychologist specializing in the treatment of adolescents with substance use disorders. She is an Assistant Professor (Research) in the Center for Alcohol and Addictions Studies at the Brown School of Public Health and the Evaluation Director of the New England Addiction Technology Transfer Center. Dr. Becker received her Ph.D. in Clinical Psychology from Duke University and completed her clinical residency at Harvard Medical School's McLean Hospital. She joined the Center for Alcohol and Addictions Studies as a postdoctoral fellow and transitioned to the faculty in 2011. Dr. Becker directs a program of research funded by the National Institute on Drug Abuse that explores novel ways to improve the treatment of adolescents with substance use disorders. She has authored over 30 peer-reviewed publications and book chapters and serves on the Editorial Board of the *Journal of Substance Abuse Treatment*.

PHOTO CREDITS